GUARDING WHAT YOU VALUE MOST

NORTH AMERICAN AEROSPACE DEFENSE COMMAND
CELEBRATING 50 YEARS

NORAD Headquarters
Peterson Air Force Base, Colorado
2008

For sale by the Superintendent of Documents, U.S. Government Printing Office
Internet: bookstore.gpo.gov   Phone: toll free (866) 512-1800;   DC area (202) 512-1800
Fax: (202) 512-2104 Mail: Stop IDCC, Washington, DC 20402-0001

ISBN 978-0-16-080436-6

TABLE OF CONTENTS

The Need for Aerospace Defense

The United States has already a Permanent Defense Agreement with the Dominion of Canada, which is so devotedly attached to the British Commonwealth and Empire. This agreement is more effective than many of those which have often been made under formal alliances.
> *-- from Sir Winston Churchill's "Iron Curtain" speech, 5 March 1946*

We face a hostile ideology — global in scope, atheistic in character, ruthless in purpose, and insidious in method. Unhappily the danger it poses promises to be of indefinite duration. To meet it successfully, there is called for, not so much the emotional and transitory sacrifices of crisis, but rather those which enable us to carry forward steadily, surely, and without complaint the burdens of a prolonged and complex struggle — with liberty the stake.
> *-- from President Dwight D. Eisenhower's farewell address, 17 January 1961*

Let every nation know, whether it wishes us well or ill, that we shall pay any price, bear any burden, meet any hardship, support any friend, oppose any foe, in order to assure the survival and the success of liberty.
> *-- from President John F. Kennedy's inaugural address, 20 January 1961*

At the same time, however, they must be made to understand we will never compromise our principles and standards. We will never give away our freedom.
> *-- from President Ronald Reagan's "Evil Empire" speech, 8 March 1983*

Let us never forget that while, on 9/11, we saw the worst evils of which humanity is capable, we also bore witness to countless acts of extraordinary human courage and compassion.
> *-- from Prime Minister Stephen Harper's speech in New York City, 20 September 2006*

Soviet Tu-95 "Bear" Long-range Bomber

NORAD
Crest and Heraldry

L'emblème et le blason du NORAD

The NORAD crest has been used since 1958.

The blue background of the shield signifies the air; the turquoise waters on the globe denote the sea; the yellow continent indicates the land – the three environments in which any defense of the North American continent would take place.

The silver wings are symbolic of the armed forces and the might of NORAD.

The sword pointing toward the northern skies represents the direction that is considered "the shortest approach of the potential aggressor." When we consider the newer terrorist threat, we may consider that the sharp edges of the sword are prepared to meet any aggressor in our domestic airspace.

Two yellow lightning bolts discharging from the sword portray the instantaneous striking power with which NORAD is prepared to meet any aggressor.

Depuis la formation du NORAD le 12 mai 1958, l'emblème du NORAD a été fièrement affiché en tant que symbole d'unité entre les États-Unis et le Canada.

Le fond bleu du bouclier représente l'air; les eaux turquoise sur le globe désignent l'océan; le continent jaune évoque la terre - ceux-ci représentent les trois environnements dans lesquels toute opération de défense du continent nord-américain prendrait place.

Les ailes d'argent sont symboliques des forces armées et de la puissance du NORAD.

L'épée, pointant vers les cieux nordiques, représente la direction considérée comme "l'approche la plus courte d'un agresseur potentiel." Avec la venue de nouvelles menaces terroristes, nous pouvons aussi dire que les bords coupants de l'épée sont prêts à faire face à tout agresseur, à l'intérieur de notre espace aérien.

Les deux éclairs jaunes, jaillissant de l'épée, symbolisent la force de frappe instantanée, avec laquelle le NORAD réagirait, face à n'importe quel agresseur.

F-102 "Delta Dagger" and CF-100 "Canuck" on NORAD patrol

Counterclockwise from Top: NORAD Headquarters (Bldg 2) Peterson AFB, CO; Ent AFB, CO; Ent Bldg (Bldg 1470) Peterson AFB, CO; CANR Headquarters, Canada; North Portal, CMAFS, CO

NORAD
NORTH AMERICAN AEROSPACE DEFENSE COMMAND

The North American Aerospace Defense Command (NORAD) is a binational United States and Canadian organization charged with the missions of aerospace warning and aerospace control for North America. Aerospace warning includes the monitoring of man-made objects in space and the detection, validation, and warning of attack against North America whether by aircraft, missiles, or space vehicles, through mutual support arrangements with other commands. Aerospace control includes ensuring air sovereignty and air defense of the airspace of Canada and the United States. The May 2006 NORAD Agreement renewal added a maritime warning mission, which entails a shared awareness and understanding of the activities conducted in U.S. and Canadian maritime approaches, maritime areas and inland waterways.

To accomplish these critically important missions, NORAD continually adjusts its structure to meet the demands of a changing world. The commander is appointed by, and is responsible to, both the US president and the Canadian prime minister. The commander maintains his headquarters at Building 2, Peterson Air Force Base (AFB), CO. NORAD's original headquarters location was established at Ent AFB near downtown Colorado Springs in 1957. By the time Ent AFB closed in 1976, the NORAD Headquarters had moved to the Ent Building at Peterson AFB. The headquarters was transferred from the Ent Building to Building 2 in 2002. The NORAD and US Northern Command (USNORTHCOM) Command Center serves as a central collection and coordination facility for a worldwide system of sensors designed to provide the commander and the leadership of Canada and the U.S. with an accurate picture of any aerospace threat. Three subordinate regional headquarters are located at Elmendorf AFB, AK; Canadian Forces Base, Winnipeg, Manitoba; and Tyndall AFB, FL. These headquarters receive direction from the commander and control air operations within their respective areas of responsibility.

To accomplish the aerospace warning mission, the commander of NORAD provides an integrated tactical warning and attack assessment to the governments of Canada and the United States. To accomplish the aerospace control mission, NORAD uses a network of satellites, ground-based radar, airborne radar and fighters to detect, intercept and, if necessary, engage any air-breathing threat to North America. As a part of its aerospace control mission, NORAD assists in the detection and monitoring of aircraft suspected of illegal drug trafficking. This information is passed to civilian law enforcement agencies to help combat the flow of illegal drugs into North America. The command is currently implementing the new maritime warning mission.

Through outstanding binational cooperation, NORAD has proven itself effective in its roles of watching, warning, and responding. NORAD continues to play an important role in the defense of Canada and the US by evolving to meet the changing threat. The events of September 11, 2001 demonstrated NORAD's continued relevance to North American security. Today, NORAD provides civil authorities with a potent military response capability to counter domestic airspace threats.

While the national leadership of Canada and the U.S. continue to refine our response to the terrorist threat, NORAD's proven abilities and unique capabilities will remain a vital part of homeland defense.

As we celebrate this significant milestone in NORAD's history, I am honored to be part of this uniquely binational military organization. NORAD's existence and evolution are a testament to our enduring relationship and the deeply shared values of defending our homelands.

Never has the role of defending our homelands been more important than in recent years as we experienced unimagined terrorist activities in the skies within our own borders. To guard our nations, the Command continually adapts to meet new and emerging threats.

The men and women of NORAD have earned great respect worldwide since the Command was created half a century ago. I am especially proud of our alert forces, who serve with tireless dedication, 24 hours a day, 7 days a week, 365 days a year. They have never faltered in the discharge of their duty of standing watch - guarding our loved ones, our communities and our way of life.

As you read this book, I hope you enjoy the walk through NORAD history, commemorating our role in keeping our nations safe for half a century. On the occasion of our fiftieth anniversary, please join me in a salute to the members of NORAD, past and present.

Alors que nous célébrons cet événement marquant dans l'histoire du NORAD, je suis honoré de faire partie de cette organisation militaire binationale unique. L'existence et l'évolution du NORAD témoignent de nos relations solides ainsi que des valeurs profondes que nous partageons en ce qui a trait à la défense de nos patries.

Au cours des dernières années, la défense de nos patries n'a jamais joué un rôle aussi important que depuis les événements terroristes inimaginables survenus dans nos espaces aériens intérieurs. Ainsi, pour veiller sur nos nations, le commandement du NORAD s'adapte continuellement pour faire face aux nouvelles menaces qui surgissent.

Depuis la création du commandement, il y a un demi-siècle, les hommes et les femmes du NORAD demeurent un modèle d'excellence, qui leur vaut une marque de respect absolue, partout dans le monde. Je suis particulièrement fier de nos unités en état d'alerte qui nous servent sans répit, 24 heures par jour, sept jours par semaine, 365 jours par année. Ils n'ont jamais failli dans l'exercice de leurs fonctions, maintenant la garde et protégeant ceux que nous aimons, nos communautés, nos mœurs et tout ce qui nous tient à coeur.

En lisant ce livre, j'espère que vous pourrez apprécier le cheminement du NORAD au fil des ans, lequel commémore son jubilé et son rôle essentiel à protéger nos nations.

À l'occasion de notre cinquantième anniversaire, je vous invite à vous joindre à moi pour saluer les membres du NORAD, d'hier et d'aujourd'hui.

General
Victor E. Renuart, Jr.
Commander
NORAD
and USNORTHCOM

Over the past 50 years, we have watched our world transform from one of Cold War anxiety to one of terrorist attacks in our own backyards. As Deputy Commander of NORAD, I am honoured to be part of this military organization where Canadian and American troops have long stood shoulder-to-shoulder in countering these threats – and continue their vigilance as we adapt to this changing world.

This role of guarding the things we all value most is one that the men and women of NORAD carry out with pride. From dawn to dusk, and through the long, dark nights, they are the "ardent sentries" who ensure that our citizens enjoy peace behind a "vigilant shield." These terms I've used in quotation marks are the titles we have given to the two major exercises we conduct each year – exercises that ensure our readiness. They aptly describe our devout duty, just as the name of our daily mission, "OPERATION NOBLE EAGLE," exemplifies the swift and sure actions we take to defend our homelands.

I am proud of this Command's history and of the way it continues to evolve to meet the challenges we face. Alongside General Renuart, I also hope you will join in saluting those who serve in NORAD.

Lors des 50 dernières années, nous avons été témoin d'une transformation à l'échelle mondiale, passant de l'anxiété de la guerre froide aux attaques terroristes frappant à nos portes. En tant que commandant adjoint du NORAD, je suis honoré d'être compté parmi cette organisation militaire, où les troupes canadiennes et américaines se sont épaulées sans relâche pour contrer ces menaces et continuent d'être vigilantes tout en s'adaptant à ce monde en perpétuel changement.

Être gardien de ce qui nous tient à cœur est un rôle que les hommes et les femmes du NORAD accomplissent avec fierté. De l'aube au crépuscule, lors de longues et sombres nuits, ils sont les sentinelles dévouées - « ardent sentries » - qui permettent à nos citoyens de jouir d'une paix continuelle derrière un bouclier vigilant - « vigilant shield ». Ces termes, cités entre guillemets, sont les appellations que nous avons données à nos deux exercices majeurs que nous exécutons chaque année et qui assurent notre état de capacité opérationnelle. Ces termes décrivent judicieusement notre dévouement face à notre devoir, tout comme le nom de notre mission quotidienne, « Opération Noble Eagle », qui exemplifie les actions rapides et indubitables que nous prenons pour défendre nos patries.

Je suis fier de l'histoire de ce commandement et de la façon dont il continue à évoluer pour faire face aux défis qui surgissent. De concert avec le Général Renuart, j'espère aussi que vous vous joindrez à nous pour honorer ceux et celles qui servent au sein du NORAD.

**Lieutenant-General
Charlie Bouchard
Deputy Commander
NORAD**

Cheyenne Mountain Command Center

NORAD DECADE HIGHLIGHTS

16 Feb 51

The Joint Chiefs of Staff (JCS) approved a US-Canadian Permanent Joint Board on Defense (PJBD) recommendation (51/1) for an extension of the Permanent Radar Net. It called for the extension and consolidation of the present control and warning system of Canada and the US into one operational system to meet air defense needs of both countries.

10 Mar 51

US Army Antiaircraft Command assumed command for the first time of all antiaircraft forces assigned to air defense.

14 Jul 52

Start of US Ground Observer Corps Operation Skywatch, during which civilian observer posts were manned 24 hours per day.

Soviet Tu-95 "Bear" long-range bomb

1951   1952   1953   1954

24 Feb 54

President Eisenhower approved the National Security Council's recommendation for construction of a Distant Early Warning (DEW) Line.

1 Sep 54

Continental Air Defense Command (CONAD) established.

Distant Early Warning (DEW) Line

1950s

30 Jul 55

First west coast US Navy picket ship station manned on a full-time basis.

Jan 58

Mid-Canada [radar] Line declared fully operational.

Jan 58

US Ground Observer Corps reduced from 24-hour to ready-reserve status.

US Navy picket ship

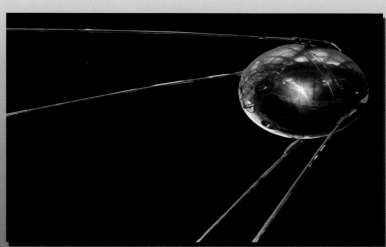

Model of Soviet satellite Sputnik I

1955   **1956**   **1957**   **1958**

21 Mar 57

The US Army Antiaircraft Command was redesignated Army Air Defense Command (ARADCOM).

15 Jul 57

The main DEW Line from Cape Dyer, Baffin Island to Cape Lisburne, AK declared technically ready.

1 Aug 57

East and West portions of the DEW Line placed under operational control of Uinted States Air Force (USAF) Air Defense Command and Alaskan Air Command, respectively.

1 Aug 57

The Canadian Minister of National Defence and the US Secretary of Defense jointly announced the agreement between their governments to establish integrated operational control of the air defense forces of the two countries.

27 Aug 57

Soviet Union announced successful launch of a multi-stage ballistic missile.

Aug 57

DEW Line was dedicated by US Air Force.

12 Sep 57

North American Air Defense Command (NORAD) was established with headquarters at Ent Air Force Base in Colorado Springs, CO. Commander-in-Chief, NORAD assigned operational control over Canadian and US air defense forces. CINCNORAD dual-hatted as Commander-in-Chief, CONAD [US joint command].

4 Oct 57

Sputnik I, the first man-made satellite, was launched by the USSR.

Nov 57

The first Baker-Nunn precision optical satellite tracking camera installed at White Sands, NM.

14 Jan 58

United States announced decision to establish a Ballistic Missile Early Warning System (BMEWS.)

12 May 58

The agreement between the US and Canadian governments establishing NORAD was formalized. The agreement included 11 principles governing the organization and operation of NORAD and called for a renewal of the agreement in 10 years.

AMERICA NEEDS <u>YOU</u> IN THE GROUND OBSERVER CORPS!

The potential of modern military offense is such that a surprise raid against this country could cause tremendous casualties.

Our military defense is aware of this possibility. Air Force interceptor planes and Army antiaircraft batteries are designed to repel such an attack.

But—if that attack ever comes—*warning must come through in time!* Citizen volunteer plane spotters—ground observers—play a vital role in providing the necessary warning.

Already some 300,000 civilian Americans are contributing to the job of guarding our ramparts. I salute these Ground Observers for their patience, their perseverance, their patriotism.

But the job calls for twice their number to man these vital posts. Will you serve your country for 2 hours a week?

Dwight D. Eisenhower

PRESIDENT OF THE UNITED STATES

© MURAY

1958   1959

CINCNORAD Gen Partridge and NORAD Deputy, Air Marshal Slemon

Jun 58

First ARADCOM unit became operational with Nike Hercules, Battery A, 2d Missile Battalion, 57th Artillery, near Chicago.

Jul 58

Pacific Sea Barrier, consisting of US Navy picket ships, became fully operational.

31 Jul 58

CINCNORAD recommended to the JCS that a hardened combat operations center with adjacent headquarters complex for NORAD be constructed without delay in the Colorado Springs area.

2 Aug 58

The first two stations (one for transmission and one for receiving) of an electronic fence across the southern US, the US Navy's space surveillance system (NAVSPASUR), became operational.

Jan 59

JS Ground Observer Corps inactivated.

26 Jan 59

First Semi-Automatic Ground Environment (SAGE) Division became operational.

18 Mar 59

The JCS approved locating a new NORAD Combat Operations Center in Cheyenne Mountain, south of Colorado Springs, CO.

1 Apr 59

The Aleutian extension of the DEW Line (DEW West) became operational.

Apr 59

Texas Tower No. 4 became operational, completing the off-shore radar platform program as part of NORAD's air defense networks.

31 May 59

CINCNORAD told JCS that he firmly believed NORAD should be designated the military command to operate the National Space Surveillance Control Center and he was proceeding with planning for its future integration into the new, hardened Combat Operations Center in Cheyenne Mountain.

DEW Line radar stations located in Alaska

1959

1960

25 Mar 60

US Navy picket ships were withdrawn from the Atlantic DEW Line sea barrier.

22 Jul 60

The Commander, USAF Air Defense Command, supported the development of a space-based Missile Defense Alarm System (MIDAS) and stated it was imperative to expand and accelerate the program to meet the Intercontinental Balistic Missile (ICBM) threat.

Sep 60

Exercise Sky Shield is the first continent-wide exercise under NORAD direction and the first grounding of all non-exercise air traffic in US and Canada.

Sep 60

BMEWS Site No. 1, Thule Air Base, Greenland, detection radars reached initial operational capability – first operation of BMEWS.

7 Nov 60

Space Detection and Tracking System (SPADATS) transferred to NORAD operational control and operational command to CONAD.

"Texas Tower" sea-based radar platform

1 Feb 61

NAVSPASUR assigned to SPADATS under operational control of CINCNORAD.

14 Feb 61

1st Aerospace Surveillance and Control Squadron activated at Ent AFB, CO to operate the SPADATS Center. The squadron was also responsible for operation of the BMEWS Central Computer and Display Facility in the NORAD Operations Center.

16 Jun 61

Excavation began for the NORAD Combat Operations Center in Cheyenne Mountain.

3 Jul 61

Space Detection and Tacking System (SPADATS) Center officially dedicated at Ent Air Force Base, CO.

1 Aug 61

Four sites of the Greenland extension (DEW East) of the DEW Line became operational. This completed the entire DEW Line from Greenland to the Aleutians.

16 June 61: First blast to begin construction at Cheyenne Mountain Complex

1961

1962

Sep 61

BMEWS Site No. 2, Clear Air Station, AK, achieved full operational capability.

14 Oct 61

"The Day the Planes Stood Still." Exercise Sky Shield II grounded all civilian aircraft for 12 hours by special FAA order. It was the largest airborne military exercise ever: 1,800 NORAD fighters flew 6,000 sorties. An estimated 2,900 commercial flights were delayed.

Feb 62

Alaskan NORAD Region Headquarters organized.

8 Feb 62

General L. S. Kuter, CINCNORAD, briefed President Kennedy and Vice President Johnson on the adequacy of continental defense. He advocated extending the missile warning system to cover approaches by missiles from any direction.

President John F. Kennedy and Gen Laurence S. Kuter

19 Jul 62

A Nike Zeus antiballistic missile (ABM) made first successful interception of an ICBM target nose cone, flown at true ICBM range, speed, and trajectory of Kwajalein. The target was boosted into trajectory by an Atlas missile launched from Vandenberg AFB, CA.

6 Aug 62

Secretary of Defense Robert McNamara directed the USAF to drop all plans for deploying MIDAS, an early forerunner system for infrared missile warning, and to reorganize the program as an R&D effort.

Oct 62

CONAD increases its weapons readiness status because of Cuban Missile Crisis. CONAD also increased its radar and weapons forces in the Florida area and dispersed part of interceptor force in US.

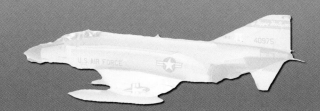

Nike "Hercules" antiballistic missiles

1963   **1964**   **1965**

17 Aug 63

Canada agreed to permit the use of nuclear warheads on BOMARC IM-99Bs based in Canada.

BOMARC IM-99Bs

Jan 64

BMEWS Site No. 3, Fylingdales Moor, England, became operational.

23 Jul 64

BOMARC IM-99A phased out of USAF Air Defense Command's inventory as a tactical weapon.

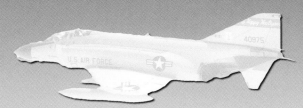

1 Sep 65

Naval Forces Continental Air Defense Command disestablished, although Navy representation at CONAD/NORAD headquarters, the regions, and sectors continued.

20 Apr 66

CINCNORAD transferred the NORAD Combat Operations Center operations from Ent Air Force Base to the Cheyenne Mountain Complex.

2 May 66

NORAD informed HQ USAF that during the fiscal years 1970-1972 it would need to completely redesign the NORAD Combat Operations Center system (425L). It reasoned that by Fiscal Year (FY) 1971 computers and peripheral equipment in the center would be eight years old and obsolete.

From top to bottom, F-4 "Phantom" and F-5 "Freedom Fighter"

1966　　　　　　**1967**　　　　　　**1968**

1960s

Cheyenne Mountain Complex 12

6 Feb 67

Space Defense Center became operational in Cheyenne Mountain Complex. The NORAD Combined Operations Center achieved full operational capability in Cheyenne Mountain. The total cost for the project to that date was $142.4M.

Cheyenne Mountain Complex 25-ton blast door

30 Mar 68

Canada and the US renewed the NORAD Agreement through an exchange of diplomatic notes. The renewal became effective 12 May 68. Three important changes were made in the original agreement signed in May 58:

(1) The renewal period would run for 5 years instead of 10 years.

(2) The 1968 agreement provided for termination of the agreement upon request of either government following a period of notice of one year.

(3) The first agreement had made no mention of defense against ballistic missiles, but the 1968 agreement specifically affirmed that Canada would not be committed to participate in an active ballistic missile defense.

Soviet SS-X-15 ICBM

1969 — **1970**

AN/FPS-85 phased-array RADAR site at Eglin AFB, FL

Jun 69

The US Senate Armed Services Committee approved authorization of $759,100,000 for the Safeguard System.

20 Jun 69

HQ USAF issued System Management Directive 9-312-427M(1), "Cheyenne Mountain Complex Improvement Program (427M)."

25 Jul 69

The US Army redesignated the Sentinel System, the US ABM missile defense system, as the Safeguard System.

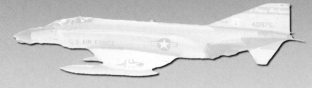

May 70

The AN/FPS-85 phased-array detection and tracking radar at Eglin Air Force Base, FL, was declared fully operational. This did not include the SLBM detection and warning function.

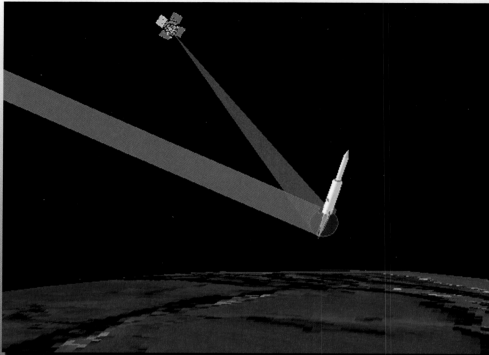

Mar 71

Twenty-seven Nike Hercules batteries in the US released from air defense alert and inactivated on 30 Jun 71.

Oct 71

The first successful synchronous orbit of a Defense Suport Program (DSP) satellite, capable of providing space-based missile early warning.

26 May 72

A "Treaty Between the United States of America and the Union of Soviet Socialist Republics on the Limitation of Anti-Ballistic Missile Systems" was concluded. Treaty ratified by US Senate on 3 Aug 72. It limited antiballistic missile deployment in each country to two sites, one for defense of the national capital, and one for defense against ICBMs.

10 May 73

By an exchange of notes, Canada and the US extended the NORAD Agreement without alteration for a period of two years to 12 May 1975.

Illustration of DSP satellites detecting a missile heat signature

1971   1972   1973

1970s

Illustration of DSP satellite

4 Mar 74

Secretary of Defense Schlesinger, in the Annual Defense Department Report, FY 75, said assured capability to retaliate decisively against Soviet cities even after absorbing the full weight of a Soviet nuclear attack offered the best hope of deterring attack, thus protecting our cities. Therefore, spending $1B a year on air defenses was no longer consistent with overall US strategic policy. This concept is popularly known as "Mutually Assured Destruction" (MAD).

31 Mar 74

The Safeguard ABM site at Grand Forks, ND achieved initial operational capability. This was the nation's first and only ABM site. Operational command was assigned to CINC Continental Air Defense Command in Apr 75 and achieved full operational capability in Oct 75. The site closed in Feb 76.

Jan 75

US Army Air Defense Command, component command of NORAD/CONAD, inactivated at Ent AFB, CO.

Apr 75

CINCCONAD assumed operational control of Safeguard.

14

CF-101 "Voodoos"

30 Jun 75
CONAD, created 1 Sep 54, was disestablished.

1 Jul 75
The JCS reorganized the Aerospace Defense Command into a specified command. Designated ADCOM, it retained its identity as a USAF component, while assuming those functions formerly exercised by CONAD.

18 Jul 75
The FPS-85 radar at Eglin AFB FL, formerly a space surveillance radar, was modified to perform the sea-launched ballistic missile detection and tracking function. It achieved initial operational capability on this date.

Aug 75
First of new series of quarterly NORAD exercises, Vigilant Overview 76-1, was conducted.

1974   **1975**

---

8 May 75
In an exchange of notes, Canada and the US extended the NORAD Agreement for five years. Principal features of the renewal agreement were:

- Recognition that ballistic missiles constituted the primary threat to North America
- The ballistic missile caveat remained in the agreement (Canada would not commit to participation in missile defense program)
- Need to monitor space activities of both strategic and tactical interest for defense of North America
- Need to maintain effective surveillance of airspace to ensure air sovereignity of both nations

12 May 75
NORAD Agreement renewal acknowledged role of NORAD in space surveillance and aerospace warning of attack.

Sep 75
USAF approved the tethered balloon radar (Seek Skyhook) system at Cudjoe Key Air Station, FL.

Sep 75
Canada's military air services organized into a single command – Canadian Forces Air Command.

SIC ITUR AD ASTRA

Canadian Forces (CF) Air Command

10 Feb 76

Aerospace Defense Command, acting on JCS orders, informed all concerned that Safeguard ABM System operations were terminated and that the system was released from operational control to Commander in Chief, Aerospace Defense Command.

Apr 76

PAVE PAWS, a phased-array early warning radar proposed to replace Sea-Launched Ballistic Missile warning system radars (AN/FSS-7s), contract awarded for site at Otis AFB, MA, and at Beale AFB, CA.

Aug 76

Safeguard ABM system inactivated and Safeguard assets transferred to US Army Ballistic Missile Defense Systems Command.

31 Aug 76

A Canadian Space Detection and Tracking System Site at St. Margarets, New Brunswick, reached initial operational capability. It had one Baker-Nunn satellite tracking camera and one satellite identification and tracking telescope.

Phased-array radar

1976

1977

USAF E-3 AWACS

Oct 76

System testing of new Cobra Dane phased-array radar began at Shemya AFB, AK. Cobra Dane supported Spacetrack and other missions.

Dec 76

Two E-3A Airborne Warning and Control Systems (AWACS) aircraft participated in a NORAD-wide exercise, Vigilant Overview 77-1, flying in the 25th NORAD Region area of responsibility. This demonstrated for the first time the ability of the E-3A force to execute the air defense mission in a North American environment.

Dec 76

The Perimeter Acquisition Radar (PAR), Langdon, ND reached initial operational capability. PAR is part of the PAR Attack Characterization System (PARCS) which is the only operating system remaining from the Safeguard ABM System. PARCS was integrated into the NORAD Combat Operations System on 4 Jan 77.

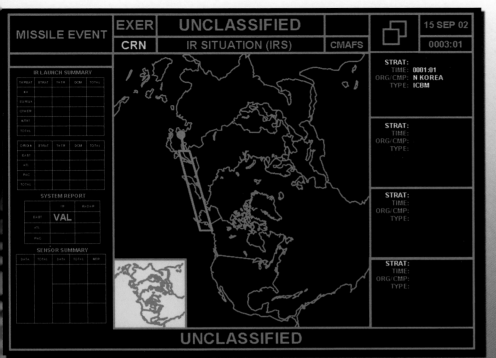

Command Center Processing and Display System Replacement (CCPDSR)

1 Oct 79

The first of a two-part reorganization of aerospace defense and surveillance and warning resources took place with the transfer of USAF ADCOM atmospheric defense resources (interceptors and warning radars) to the Tactical Air Command (TAC), and communications and electronics assets to the Air Force Communications Command (AFCC). Thereafter, these two commands had resource management responsibility.

9 Nov 79

For about three minutes, a test scenario of a missile attack on North America was inadvertently transmitted to the operational side of the 427M system in the Cheyenne Mountain Complex Operations Center. It was processed as real information, displayed on missile warning consoles in the command post, and transmitted to national command centers. About eight minutes elapsed between the time test data appeared and NORAD assessed confidence that no strategic attack was underway. This aroused widespread public and congressional interest. Corrective actions to prevent a reoccurrence continued into 1980. This incident was fictionalized and exaggerated in the 1983 movie *WarGames*.

1978 — 1979 — 1980

29 Jan 79

The first E-3A AWACS aircraft was designated to support NORAD mission requirements. This marked the beginning of the changeover from the (SAGE) system to the Joint Surveillance System (JSS) radar configuration in the 25th NORAD Region.

29 Mar 79

The USAF made a public announcement of its plans to reorganize its aerospace defense forces. Consequently, the USAF inactivated ADCOM as a major command and reassigned its resources to other commands.

Apr 79

Last US Army Nike Hercules and Hawk batteries dedicated to continental air defense were deactivated.

1 Dec 79

The second part of the USAF ADCOM reorganization took place with the transfer of missile warning and space surveillance assets to Strategic Air Command (SAC).

Apr 80

Six of seven FSS-7 Sea-Launched Ballistic Missile detection sensor sites phased out. Site at MacDill AFB, FL, retained.

3 & 6 Jun 80

Failure of a computer chip within the NORAD Control System caused false missile warning data to be transmitted to SAC, the National Command Center, and the National Alternate Command Center. This incident built upon the public and congressional concern dating to 9 Nov 79.

Jan 81
USAF published the Air Defense Master Plan recommending new initiatives in Air Defense.

Mar 81
President Ronald Reagan and Prime Minister Pierre Trudeau finalized the US-Canada Joint Policy Statement on Air Defense.

12 May 81
Canada and the US extended the NORAD Agreement for another five years. The renewal was preceded by extensive Canadian public discussion and reports on the status of the agreement. Opinion weighed heavily on the side of continued participation and that Canada should consider participation in space-based programs and systems. Changes in the agreement reflected this interest:

- The ballistic missile defense caveat was dropped.
- The term change from "air defense" to "aerospace defense" was agreed upon.
- Continued effort was to be made to realign regional boundaries.
- Wording changes to indicate importance of space to North American defense and need for enchanced cooperation in space surveillance activities were made.

USAF F-16 Fighte

1981   **1982**   **1983**

1980S

Baker-Nunn camera used to photograph satellites in space

31 May 81
The Canadian satellite tracking unit ceased operations at Cold Lake, Alberta. The site had been equipped with a Baker-Nunn Camera.

Oct 81
HQ Cheyenne Mountain Support Group, a unit assigned to the Aerospace Defense Center, was activated at the Cheyenne Mountain Complex.

1 Sep 82
USAF Space Command activated and given resource management of missile warning and space surveillance assets which was under operational control of ADCOM.

1 Jun 83
The 22nd NORAD Region was redesignated as the Canadian NORAD Region with headquarters at North Bay, Ontario, Canada.

Canadian Forces Base North Bay in Ontario, Canada

1984   1985

18 Mar 85

Secretary of Defense Caspar W. Weinberger, and the Canadian Minister of Defence, Erik Nielsen, signed the North American Air Defense Modernization Memorandum, which authorized the building of North Warning System (NWS).

2 Aug 85

The Chairman of the Joint Chiefs of Staff (CJCS) approved the organizational structure for US Space Command (USSPACECOM), a JCS unified command, inactivation of ADCOM, and USSPACECOM's relationship with NORAD, and proposed establishment of US Element NORAD (USELMNORAD).

28 Aug 85

President Reagan advised Canadian Prime Minister Mulroney of US plans for activating the USSPACECOM.

7 Sep 85

Canadian Government announced its decision to decline the US invitation to participate in the research stage of the Strategic Defense Initiative (SDI).

16 Sep 85

US Secretary of Defense directed the Unified Command Plan (UCP) be amended to reflect establishment of USSPACECOM and USELMNORAD.

23 Sep 85

USSPACECOM was activated at Colorado Springs, CO. Component commands were Air Force Space Command, Naval Space Command, and the Army Space Liaison Office. One of USSPACECOM's mission taskings was to support NORAD by providing missile warning and space surveillance data as necessary to fulfill the US's commitment to the NORAD Agreement.

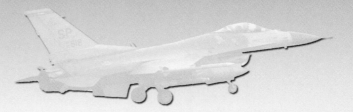

19

27 Jan 87

The Canadian Chief of Defence Staff validated the Wide Area Surveillance System NORAD Statement of Requirement (NSOR.)

2 Mar 87

USSPACECOM's Space Operations Center (SPOC), located at Peterson AFB, achieved initial operational capability.

Apr 87

The US and Canada began deployment of the first segment of the NWS. The NWS series of radar sites replaced the DEW Line.

24 Jun 87

The solid-state phased-array radar at Thule Air Base, Greenland, achieved initial operational capability.

1986

1987

19 Mar 86

Canadian Prime Minister Mulroney and President Reagan signed the NORAD renewal agreement. It became effective on 12 May 1986.

1 Oct 86

Continental United States (CONUS) NORAD Region activated.

19 Dec 86

Aerospace Defense Command, the specified command, was inactivated at Colorado Springs, CO.

Phased-array radar at Thule Air Base, Greenland

The Berlin Wall and Brandenburg Gate (June 1987), two years before being dismantled

2 Nov 88

Deputy Secretary of Defense, William H. Taft, IV, granted CINCNORAD full and permanent membership in the Department of Defense Planning, Programming, and Budgeting System to better ensure NORAD resource requirements were addressed.

24 Jan 89

Government of Canada formally agreed with NORAD's involvement in anti-drug mission as being the NORAD Agreement air sovereignty mission.

15 Oct 89

CINCNORAD published counternarcotics campaign plan, SNOWFENCE 90, detailing overall doctrine, strategy and force employment plans in support of national anti-drug efforts.

Nov 89

The fall of the Berlin Wall heralded the beginning of the end of the Cold War.

1988   **1989**   **1990**

16 - 27 May 88

The US First Air Force and Air Command (Canadian Forces) conducted site surveys of the five Forward Operating Locations in Canada.

30 Jun 88

NORAD implemented a new Air Defense Identification Zone (ADIZ) in order to make the ADIZ contiguous around the periphery of North America. The ADIZ was defined as that area of airspace over land or water in which the ready identification, location, and control of aircraft was required in the interest of national security.

22 Jul 88

The detection and tracking BMEWS Site No. 1 (Thule) was dismantled after having been replaced by phased-array radar in 1987.

28 Sep 88

National Defense Authorization Act for FY 1989 Directed Department of Defense involvement in drug interdiction enforcement.

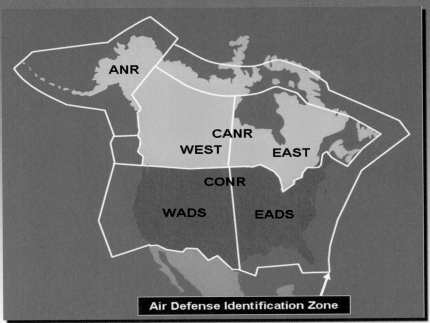

NORAD Regions and Sectors

Jan 91

As a result of the continued US and Allied presence in the Middle East resulting from Operations DESERT SHIELD and DESERT STORM, NORAD's Missile Correlation Center added Theater Missile Warning to its mission set.

23 Jan 91

Fighter Group Canadian Regional HQ proposed an upgrade of the Regional Operational Command Centers (ROCC).

May 91

The USSPACECOM J4-J6 staff prepared a draft NORAD/USSPACECOM regulation that outlined the NORAD/USSPACECOM Integrated Command and Control System Mission Systems Integration process.

2 May 91

Phase I, Precision Acquisition Vehicle Entry Phased Array Warning System (PAVE PAWS) radar upgrade program, at Beale AFB in California, acheived initial operational capability.

23 Sep 91

CINCNORAD dedicated NORAD/USSPACECOM Combined Intelligence Center (CIC), marking the culmination of efforts to consolidate the intelligence resources of the two commands.

US Forces secure an Iraqi SCUD missile

1991

1992

Cheyenne Mountain Command Center

7-17 Jan 92

Operation Sunburst, a joint US Customs Service/Department of Defense counternarcotics operation was conducted.

11 Feb 92

The Secretary of the Air Force concurred with CINCNORAD's request to continue operation of the east coast OTH-B radar on a limited basis through FY93 and maintain the west coast OTH-B site in warm storage.

Jul 92

HQ NORAD completed its Strategy Review Report outlining potential changes for the command in the future.

5 Oct 92

General Charles A. Horner, CINCNORAD, outlined his concept for NORAD participation in the ballistic missile defense program.

Feb 93

CINCNORAD General Horner issued a paper titled "Shaping NORAD in the Post-Soviet Threat," which evaluated emerging threats and how the command would defend against those dangers.

Feb 93

CINCNORAD announced the implementation of a "flexible alert" concept. The strategy gave regional commanders the authority to raise and lower readiness in their alert fighter force according to the perceived threat. This marked a radical change from 24-hour alert status performed by NORAD alert fighters during the Cold War.

Mar 93

Relocatable Over-the-Horizon (ROTHR) radar entered counter-drug operations.

Jul 93

CINCNORAD approved First Air Force and Air Combat Command's recommendation to consolidate Northwest and Southwest Sector Operations Command Centers (SOCCs) into West SOCC at McChord Air Force Base, Washington.

US Special Forces conducting counter-drug operations

1993

15 Jul 93

The DEW Line officially closed.

Nov 93

The Deputy Secretary of Defense issued Interim National Drug Control Policy. The Memorandum announced a major shift in focus for US counterdrug efforts from "transit zones" to "source countries." The policy meant a reduction in NORAD's counter-drug mission efforts.

Nov 93

Canadian and US representatives met in Washington, DC, to begin consideration of the 1996 NORAD Agreement Renewal process. Revamping the agreement to reflect the decline of the Soviet Union and the inclusion of Ballistic Missile Defense in the NORAD Agreement were major issues.

US Navy F-18 "Hornet" taking-off from Naval carrier

Mar 94

US Secretary of Defense authorized warm storage of OTH-B radar at Bangor, Maine.

1 Jan 95

NORAD combined the Northwest and Southwest Air Defense Sectors into the Western Air Defense Sector.

Artist's rendition of OTH-B radar

Two CF-18 "Hornets"

1994　　　　　　*1995*　　　　　　*1996*

16 Mar 96

CINCNORAD directed a change in names of the Region and Sector Operations Control Centers (ROCC/SOCC) to Region and Sector Air Operations Centers (RAOC/SAOC) to put them in line with Joint and USAF doctrine.

28 Mar 96

Canada and the US signed a renewal of the NORAD Agreement that became effective on 12 May 96. The 1996 Agreement redefined the command's missions as (1) aerospace warning for North America, and (2) aerospace control for North America. A consultative mechanism was included on issues concerning aerospace defense and there was a provision that both parties agreed to sound environmental practices related to NORAD operations in accordance with joint consultations.

Apr 96

Canada announced the planned transition of Canadian NORAD Region (CANR) headquarters functions to a consoliated 1st Canadian Air Division and Canadian NORAD Region Headquarters (1CAD/CANR HQ)

19 Apr 96

Observation date of the thirtieth anniversary of the Cheyenne Mountain Complex operation.

Jan 97

CINCNORAD approved the NORAD Vision 2010 Briefing, which was developed to reflect the command's vision for 2010 and beyond to include future security challenges, missions, capabilities, and an implementation process.

1 Apr 97

Transfer of responsibilities from Region Air Operations Center, North Bay, to new CANR NORAD Region HQ in Winnipeg completed.

12 Sep 97

Fortieth anniversary of the establishment of Headquarters, North American Air Defense Command (NORAD) at Ent AFB, Colorado Springs, CO.

25 Oct 99

NORAD fighters provided emergency response to Payne Stewart's Learjet 35, which ultimately crashed with no survivors in South Dakota.

Alaskan NORAD Air Defense Sector Operations Center

1997   *1998*   *1999*   *2000*

12 May 98

Fortieth anniversary of the exchange of notes between Canada and the US for the establishment of NORAD.

Aerostats provide low-level surveillance along US southern border and in Florida

16 Jun 00

NORAD agreement extension signed by US Secretary of State Madeline Albright and Canadian Minister of Foreign Affairs Lloyd Axworthy.

Jul 00

Tethered Aerostat Radar System transferred to US Customs, effective 1 Oct 00.

6 Jul 00

Groundbreaking ceremony held for new NORAD and USSPACECOM headquarters at Peterson AFB.

Nov-Dec 00

Russian Bear Bomber flights resumed in Alaska NORAD Region area. OPERATION NORTHERN DENIAL positioned US and Canadian aircraft in forward operating bases through 15 Dec.

Apr 01
Canada-US Military Cooperation Committee confirmed validation of the Cruise Missile Defense of North America Mission Needs Statement (version 5.5).

Mar-Apr 01
NORAD Combat Operations and Air Combat Command operations staff members agreed to the three Air Operating Centers (CONR, CANR, ANR).

1 Jun 01
Joint Staff issued CJCSI2610.01A, which provided interception and destruction guidance for aircraft piracy (highjacking) incidents or requests for destruction of derelict airborne objects.

20 Jun 01
FPS-117 secondary RADAR beacons to be replaced between 2002-2005.

23 Aug 01
NORAD System Support Facility and FAA announced cooperation on Flight Plan Data Software, a data-sharing project.

29 Jan 02
Canadian Vice Chief of Defence LGen George Macdonald announced that extended collaboration between US and Canadian forces on land and sea could be modeled on NORAD.

3 Sep 02
CANUS Joint Planning Group proposed by Canadian Senate Committee on National Security and Defence.

8 Nov 02
Headquarters NORAD presented with Joint Meritorious Unit Award for defense of North America (11 Sep 01 to 10 Sep 02).

3-5 Dec 02
Canadian Minister of Foreign Affairs William Graham and US Secretary of State Colin Powell exchanged diplomatic notes establishing the Bi-National Planning Group (BPG).

1 Feb 03
NORAD-USNORTHCOM provided search support and military support to civil authorities after Space Shuttle *Columbia* disaster.

2001

2002

11 Sep 01
Terrorists highjacked four US airliners, crashing two into the World Trade Center towers, one into the Pentagon, and one into a field in rural Pennsylvania. US Joint Forces Command choped Air Force and Navy aircraft to NORAD to protect against further terrorist attacks. Aegis guided missile cruisers and destroyers were deployed to assist the Air Force and Air National Guard in defending critical CONUS airspace.

13 Sep 01
CJCS designated military operations in support of homeland security as OPERATION NOBLE EAGLE (ONE).

9 Oct 01
OPERATION EAGLE ASSIST involved deployment of five NATO E-3 AWACS aircraft to Tinker AFB in Oklahoma to support ONE.

27 Nov 01
NORAD Contingency Suite (NCS) was fielded, providing critical command and control equipment and battle management software to support contingency operations within the Continental US NORAD Region (CONR).

2000s

Since 9/11, NORAD has increased its activities protecting high-visibility events such as NASA launches and sporting events. In 2002, NORAD supported the Winter Olympics in Salt Lake City. In 2006, Super Bowl XL in Detroit was protected by US and Canadian fighters under Operation NOBLE EAGLE. In 2008, the NORAD-USNORTHCOM Color Guard was invited to participate in the opening ceremonies of Super Bowl XLII in Glendale, Arizona.

2003

26 Jan 04
Cheyenne Mountain Operations Center upgrade reported in open-source news media. Upgrade included involvement in ground-based missile defense missions.

30 Jan 04
NORAD began protective measures in support of Super Bowl XXXVIII in Houston, Texas. This mission continues in subsequent years.

17 Jun 04
CDR NORAD-USNORTHCOM General Ralph Eberhart testified before the 9/11 Commission on military response to 9/11 and NORAD support provided.

5 Aug 04
US and Canadian officials approved amendment to 1996 NORAD agreement, authorizing NORAD to make missile warning information available to US commands involved in ballistic missile defense.

2004

30 Nov 04
President Bush and Prime Minister Martin issued joint communiqué reinforcing security cooperation in the areas of intelligence sharing, border security, and combating human trafficking. NORAD Agreement was expanded to address increased security cooperation.

F-22 "Raptor" in training flight out of Tyndall AFB, FL

4 Mar 05
Ribbon-cutting ceremony officially opened the renovated command center at Cheyenne Mountain Air Force Station.

21 Jun 05
Visual Warning System (VWS) was deployed in the US National Capital Region. The VWS warns pilots who encroach on the restricted flight area.

13-21 Jul 05
NORAD protected Space Shuttle *Discovery* launch at Cape Canaveral. Mission continued for *Atlantis* (Aug-Sep 06) and *Discovery* (Dec 06).

11-15 Dec 05
CDR NORAD-USNORTHCOM ADM Timothy Keating meets with Lt. Gen. Igor Khvorov, Russian long-range bomber force commander, to discuss safety of flight for aviators of both countries.

Space Shuttle Atlantis *lifts off from Kennedy Space Center, FL*

2005

VWS with examples of pilots' visual identifications

2006

1 Feb 06
Canada Command (Canada COM) stood up to conduct routine and contingency domestic operations. A close relationship with USNORTHCOM is planned.

11-13 Apr 06
NORAD fighters intercepted and escort Russian Long-range Aircraft off the Canadian and Alaskan coasts.

12 May 06
NORAD Agreement renewed to include Maritime Warning in addition to Aerospace Warning and Aerospace Control.

28 Jul 06
CDR NORAD and USNORTHCOM ADM Timothy Keating announced plan to relocate and combine the NORAD Command Center with the USNORTHCOM Command Center at Peterson AFB. Cheyenne Mountain Operations Center is redesignated as the Cheyenne Mountain Directorate, serving as a training location and alternate command center site.

2000s

30 Sep 06
US and Canadian NORAD fighters intercepted two Russian Tu-95 "Bear" Bombers near Alaskan airspace.

11 Oct 06
NORAD aircraft responded to a Manhattan airplane crash that killed NY Yankees pitcher Cory Lidle and his flight instructor.

20 Nov 06
Northeast Air Defense Sector (NEADS) and Southeast Air Defense Sector (SEADS) combined into Eastern Air Defense Sector (EADS). Western Air Defense Sector (WADS) opened its new operations center.

May 07
General Accountability Office released report on proposal to move certain NORAD and other operational centers out of Cheyenne Mountain.

28 Jun 07
Canadian National Defence Headquarters announced a $4 billion spending plan with Lockheed Martin for 80 F-35 Lightning II Joint Strike Fighters over the course of 10 years.

16 Nov 07
The NORAD Tracks Santa mission continued to grow. By 25 Dec 07, the Website recieved more than 10 million visitors and 905 million hits from 212 countries. Over 1,000 volunteer operators staffed 100 telephones and 24 computer terminals at Peterson AFB. Operators fielded approximately 450,000 telephone calls during the entire period. Activity spiked on Christmas Eve with approximately 95,000 telephone calls and 1,000 e-mails.

22 Nov 07
On their first mission in Alaska, F-22 Raptor aircraft intercepted two Russian Bear-H Bombers.

2007 *2008*

USAF F-15 "Eagle" escorts Russian Tu-95 "Bear" bomber near Alaskan NORAD Region.

9-10 Jan 08
Canadian Minister of National Defence Peter McKay visited General Renuart, CDR NORAD and USNORTHCOM, and other command leaders to discuss future NORAD, USNORTHCOM, and Canada COM cooperation.

12 May 08
NORAD celebrates its 50th anniversary with a commemorative ceremony and burial of a time capsule. Other celebratory events include a gala ball at the Broadmoor and many distinguished visitors.

2008
Transformation of primary command center of operations from Cheyenne Mountain to the NORAD and USNORTHCOM Command Center will be completed. Cheyenne Mountain will become the NORAD and USNORTHCOM Alternate Command Center (ACC) and crew training site.

U.S. AIR FORCE
Cheyenne Mountain
Air Force Station

CHEYENNE MOUNTAIN COMPLEX

NORAD Area of Responsibility

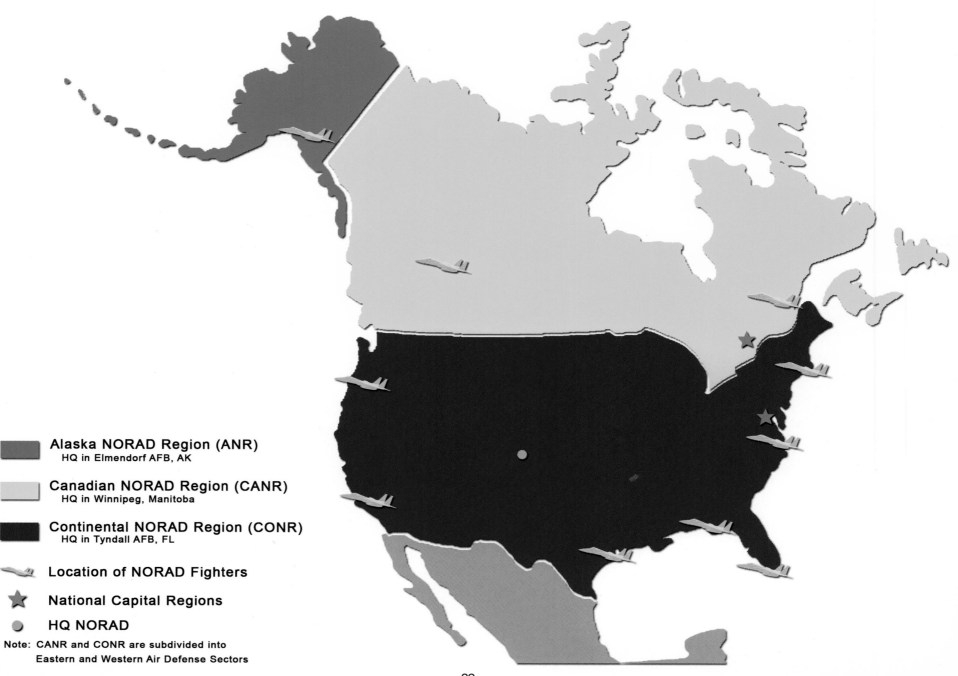

Alaska NORAD Region (ANR)
HQ in Elmendorf AFB, AK

Canadian NORAD Region (CANR)
HQ in Winnipeg, Manitoba

Continental NORAD Region (CONR)
HQ in Tyndall AFB, FL

Location of NORAD Fighters

National Capital Regions

HQ NORAD

Note: CANR and CONR are subdivided into
Eastern and Western Air Defense Sectors

Clockwise from Bottom Left: USAF E-3 AWACS, CF-18 "Hornet", Cheyenne Mountain Air Warning Center

The Air Warning Center (AWC) is the focal point for providing aerospace warning and aerospace control for North America. It provides command and control of the air surveillance and defense network, using air and ground-based radars inside and along the periphery of North America. The AWC closely monitors the airspace of Canada and the United States to detect any aircraft or cruise missiles that might violate our airspace or represent a threat.

Approximately 7,000 aircraft per day or 2.5 million aircraft a year enter Canada and the United States. Since the terrorist attacks of Sept. 11, 2001, the AWC's mission of Aerospace Warning and Aerospace Control has expanded to include the interior airspace of North America. Today, the AWC monitors approximately 5,000 aircraft flying inside Canada and the United States in addition to monitoring aircraft entering North America.

As part of this mission, a small percentage of aircraft flying inside as well as outside the borders of Canada and the United States are categorized as "unknown." It is the responsibility of the AWC to determine the identity of these unknown aircraft. For the year 2000, the total number of "unknowns" was 115. For the year 2001, the number was 676.

To accomplish this mission the center uses an array of radar systems and airborne interceptors. Most unknown tracks are subsequently identified as friendly aircraft that have erred from flight plans or used improper procedures.

AIR DOMAIN

NORTH AMERICAN AEROSPACE DEFENSE COMMAND

ICBM launch

PAVE PAWS, Cape Cod, MA

34

DEW Line - Canada

Cheyenne Mountain Missile Correlation Center

The Missile Correlation Center (MCC) uses a worldwide communications and sensor network to provide warning of missile attacks launched against North America or US forces overseas 24/7. The MCC integrates "strategic" and "theater" missions. The strategic mission focuses on missiles launched from anywhere on the globe that are a potential threat to Canada or the United States.

The theater mission is concerned with short-range missile launches that could threaten US or allied forces. The MCC also tracks space launches worldwide in support of international treaties and safety. The MCC's capability to provide timely and accurate warning has improved considerably since the Gulf War and continues to improve as new computer and communications systems are added.

MISSILE DOMAIN
NORTH AMERICAN AEROSPACE DEFENSE COMMAND

US Navy destroyer, supply ship, and aircraft carrier conduct replenishment operation

USS Normandy guided missile cruiser

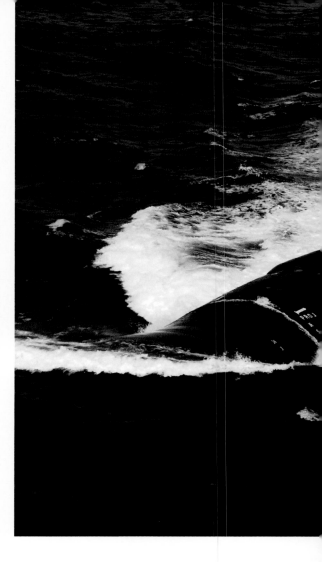

In accordance with the NORAD Agreement and Terms of Reference dated 21 February 2007, NORAD conducts the Maritime Warning mission to warn of global maritime threats to, or attacks against, North America. This mission contributes to the binational defense and security of North America by providing a strategic framework for enhancing maritime information sharing between Canada and the United States. The NORAD and USNORTHCOM Command Center's Maritime Domain watch provides strategic awareness of po-

US Navy Los Angeles-class fast attack submarine

Her Majesty's Canadian Ship (HMCS) Toronto Halifax-class frigate

tential maritime threats and enables timely and effective maritime warning to the leadership of the United States and Canada. A variety of formal and informal information sharing and exchange agreements already exist between "like-minded" agencies on both sides of the border. The NORAD Maritime Watch complements the Maritime Domain Awareness (MDA) initiatives of Canada and the United States, providing effective binational defense of our ports, coasts, and waterways.

MARITIME DOMAIN
NORTH AMERICAN AEROSPACE DEFENSE COMMAND

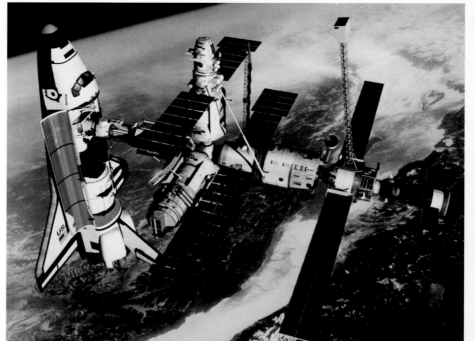

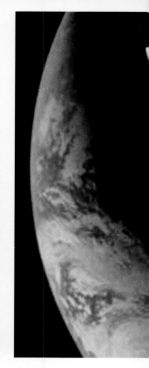

NASA rendition of Space Shuttle Atlantis docked with Russian Mir Space Station

Titan IV-B rocket launch

International Space Station as seen from Space Shuttle Atlantis

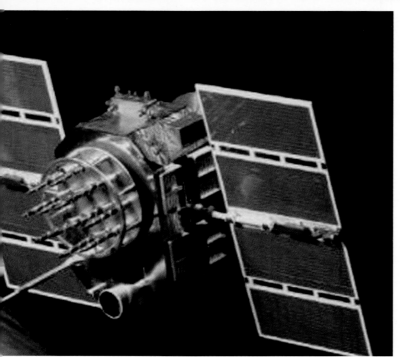

Rendition of GPS satellite in medium-earth orbit

AIR FORCE SPACE COMMAND

The US Air Force Space Command (AFSPC) Joint Space Operations Center (JSPOC) supports United States Strategic Command (USSTRATCOM) missions of surveillance and protection of US assets in space. The JSPOC's primary objective in performing the surveillance mission is to detect, track, identify, and catalog all man-made objects orbiting earth.

The JSPOC maintains a current computerized catalog of all orbiting man-made objects, charts preset positions, plots future orbital paths, and forecasts times and general locations for significant man-made objects reentering the Earth's atmosphere.

Since the launch of Sputnik in 1957, over 31,000 man-made objects have been catalogued, many of which have since re-entered the atmosphere. Currently, the JSPOC tracks over 10,000 man-made objects; approximately 20 percent of those being tracked are functioning payloads or satellites.

The JSPOC protection mission consists of electro-magnetic interference (EMI), solar phenomena, laser clearing, intentional threat, and collision avoidance. The JSPOC compiles information on hostile events that could directly or indirectly threaten US or allied space assets. This information is analyzed to determine potential impacts on assets so that timely warnings and recommendations for suitable countermeasures can be made.

NORAD operated Cheyenne Mountain's Space Control Center under US Space Command. When US Space Command was disestablished, Air Force Space Command assumed the Joint Space Operations Center mission, ultimately moving JSPOC to Vandenberg AFB in the latter half of 2007. JSPOC's mission and information are still vital to the Integrated Tactical Warning and Attack Assessment (ITW/AA) function in the NORAD Command Center.

SPACE DOMAIN
NORTH AMERICAN AEROSPACE DEFENSE COMMAND

The Command Center is the fusion point for all operations. The Command Director (CD) and crew serve as NORAD's, USNORTHCOM's, and USSTRATCOM's direct representatives for monitoring, processing, and interpreting missile, space, or air events that could threaten North America or have operational impacts on US and Canadian forces or capabilities. The operational crews come from all armed services of both nations and work together as a unified team.

The Command Center fuses data from over 40 centers with over 1,400 members worldwide and passes it to the leadership of the United States and Canada as well as regional command centers overseas.

When required, the CD must consult directly with Commander NORAD and USNORTHCOM, and Commander USSTRATCOM for time-critical assessments of missile, air, and space events. This process is known as Integrated Tactical Warning and Attack Assessment (ITW/AA).

The NORAD Combat Operations Center was located at Ent AFB in Colorado Springs from 1957 to 1966. In April 1966, the Combat Operations Center shifted operations into the newly completed Cheyenne Mountain Complex. In 2008, the NORAD and USNORTHCOM Command Center (N2C2) will assume primary watch responsibility, leaving the Cheyenne Mountain's Command Center to serve as the Alternate Command Center and training site.

Operations Centers, Old and New

Opposite, Upper Left: Canadian NORAD Region Command Center (date unknown).

Opposite, Upper Right: Canadian officers standing watch, Canadian NORAD Region (2007).

Center: NORAD Combat Operations Center at Ent AFB, Colorado (circa 1960).

Upper Left: Cheyenne Mountain Command Center (2005).

Upper Right: The new, combined NORAD and USNORTHCOM Command Center, undergoing systems installation and project completion in March 2008.

COMMAND
NORTH AMERICAN AEROSPACE DEFENSE COMMAND

New Jersey ANG F-16 fighters on ONE patrol

On 14 September, the Chairman of the Joint Chiefs of Staff designated military operations in support of homeland security as Operation NOBLE EAGLE (ONE).

For the next seven months NORAD fighters, with support from NATO airborne early warning aircraft and US Transportation Command tankers, maintained continuous Combat Air Patrol (CAP) flights over many US cities. NATO involvement fell under Operation EAGLE ASSIST. In September 2002, NORAD received the Joint Meritorious Unit Award (JMUA) for exceptionally meritorious service and achievement in the defense of North America, its actions on 9-11, and the more than 24,500 combat air patrol (CAP) sorties over the US and Canada in support of Operation NOBLE EAGLE. By comparison, during the year 2000, NORAD flew a total of 147 air defense sorties.

By October 2003, NORAD had flown more than 32,000 sorties. Over 1,500 of those sorties, which were flown by F-15 Eagles, F-16 Fighting Falcons, and Canadian CF-18s from sites throughout the US and Canada, involved targets of interest. Most of those targets were identified as pilots who mistakenly strayed into restricted airspace or whose communications or navigation equipment had failed. As ONE reached a steady-state, regular improvements included more alert bases and priorities for assets, interior radar and radio coverage, Temporary Flight Restrictions (TFR) to assist in the identification of unknown tracks, and improved interagency cooperation.

Today, ONE continues as the ongoing air patrol mission to defend North America against terrorist aggression either within or outside the nations' air borders. NORAD has responded to more than 2,700 potential airborne threats in the continental United States, Canada, and Alaska, while flying more than 45,000 sorties.

Washington Monument

NORAD 40th Anniversary F-16 flyover at Peterson AFB, CO

20th Fighter Wing F-16 over Washington, DC

ONE pilot ready for patrol

NOBLE EAGLE
NORTH AMERICAN AEROSPACE DEFENSE COMMAND

44

Remote Contiguous Communications satellite ground terminal in North Bay, Ontario

NORAD TRACKS SANTA

Volunteers answer calls and e-mails du[ring]
NORAD Tracks Sa[nta]

"NORAD Tracks Santa" Program

On 24 December 1955, a telephone call was placed to the Continental Air Defense Command (CONAD) Operations Center in Colorado Springs, CO. This call was not from the president or a general officer – rather, it was from a young boy who was following directions in a Sears advertisement printed in the local paper – he wanted to know the whereabouts of Santa Claus.

The ad featured (opposite) a photo of Santa stating: "Hey, Kiddies! Call me direct and be sure and dial the correct number." Ironically, the telephone number was printed incorrectly and rang into the CONAD Operations Center.

On duty that night was Col. Harry Shoup, who has come to be known as the "Santa Colonel." Col. Shoup received numerous calls that night and rather than hanging up, he had his operators find the location of Santa Claus on their radars and reported the information to the children.

When the North American Aerospace Defense Command (NORAD) was formed in 1958, it carried on the tradition of tracking Santa Claus. Today, using the same technology used to perform their day-to-day mission – satellites, high-powered radars and jet fighters – NORAD tracks Santa Claus as he makes his Yuletide journey around the world.

Every Christmas Eve, hundreds of volunteers – NORAD "Santa Trackers" – staff telephone hotlines and computers to answer calls and e-mails from children around the world. In addition, live updates of Santa's whereabouts are provided on the NORAD Tracks Santa Website.

In 2007, the "NORAD Tracks Santa" Website received 905 million hits from 212 countries and territories around the world. In addition, 450,000 children called the "NORAD Tracks Santa" hotline. NORAD and Santa received approximately 100,000 e-mails from children around the world inquiring of Santa's whereabouts and petitioning him with lists.

Due to the generosity of corporate and local sponsors, the "NORAD Tracks Santa" program is operated at minimal cost to the United States military.

The "NORAD Tracks Santa" program has become a magical and global phenomenon, delighting generations of families everywhere.

For more information about NORAD Tracks Santa, please visit **www.norad.mil**
Santa Hotline on Christmas Eve Only: 1-877-HI-NORAD (1-877-44-66723)

PAST NORAD COMMANDERS

**General
Earle E. Partridge
Sep 57 - Jul 59**

**General
Laurence S. Kuter
Aug 59 - Jul 62**

**General
John K. Gerhart
Aug 62 - Mar 65**

**General
Dean C. Strother
Apr 65 - Jul 66**

**General
Raymond J. Reeves
Aug 66 - Jul 69**

**General
Seth J. McKee
Aug 69 - Sep 73**

**General
Lucius D. Clay
Oct 73 - Aug 75**

**General
Daniel James, Jr.
Sep 75 - Dec 77**

**General
James E. Hill
Dec 77 - Dec 79**

**General
James V. Hartinger
Jan 80 - Jul 84**

**General
Robert T. Herres
Jul 84 - Feb 87**

**General
John L. Piotrowski
Feb 87 - Mar 90**

**General
Donald J. Kutyna
Apr 90 - Jun 92**

**General
Charles A. Horner
Jun 92 - Sep 94**

**General
Joseph W. Ashy
Sep 94 - Aug 96**

**General
Howell M. Estes, III
Aug 96 - Aug 98**

**General
Richard B. Myers
Aug 98 - Feb 00**

**General
Ralph E. Eberhart
Feb 00 - Nov 04**

**Admiral
Timothy J. Keating
Nov 04 - Mar 07**

PAST NORAD
DEPUTY COMMANDERS

Air Marshal
C. Roy Slemon
Sep 57 - Aug 64

Air Marshal
C. R. Dunlap
Aug 64 - Aug 67

Air Marshal
William R. MacBrian
Aug 67 - Jan 69

Lieutenant-General
Frederick R. Sharp
Jan 69 - Sep 69

Lieutenant-General
Edwin M. Reyno
Sep 69 - Aug 72

Lieutenant-General
Reginald J. Lane
Sep 72 - Oct 74

Lieutenant-General
Richard C. Stovel
Oct 74 - Sep 76

Lieutenant-General
David R. Adamson
Sep 76 - Aug 78

Lieutenant-General
Kenneth E. Lewis
Aug 78 - Jun 80

Lieutenant-General
Kenneth J. Thomeycroft
Jun 80 - May 83

Lieutenant-General
Donald C. Mackenzie
May 83 - Aug 86

Lieutenant-General
Donald M. McNaughton
Aug 86 - Aug 89

Lieutenant-General
Robert W. Morton
Aug 89 - Aug 92

Lieutenant-General
Brian L. Smith
Aug 92 - Aug 94

Lieutenant-General
J.D. O'Blenis
Aug 94 - Aug 95

Lieutenant-General
L.W.F. Cuppens
Aug 95 - Apr 98

Lieutenant-General
G.E.C. Macdonald
Apr 98 - Aug 01

Lieutenant-General
Kenneth R. Pennie
Aug 01 - Jul 03

Lieutenant-General
Eric A. Findley
Jul 03 - Aug 07

General Gerhart and Air Marshall Slemon brief President Kennedy during his visit to Colorado Springs in June 1963.

Prime Minister Mulroney and President Reagan sign the NORAD Agreement renewal on 19 March 1986.

NORAD Components and Command Relationships Through the Years

1954 - 1975

Established by the US Army Air Force in 1946, the Air Defense Command (ADC) formed the basis of the Continental Air Defense Command (CONAD), a joint-service command established at Ent AFB in Colorado Springs, CO, on 1 September 1954. The command supported the bi-national NORAD mission, which began on 12 September 1957, and was formalized between the US and Canada on 12 May 1958. CONAD was disestablished in 1975.

1957 - 1975

1957 - 1965

The US Army Air Defense Command (ARADCOM) served as the Army's air defense component command from 1957 to 1975. The Naval air defense component, NAVFORCONAD, served from 1957 to 1965.

1968 - 1986

1946 - 1992

The ADC was a redesignation of the Air Defense Command, dating back to 15 January 1968. In 1979, the USAF inactivated ADCOM as a major command, making it a specified command and reassigning its resources.

The ADC's atmospheric defense resources (interceptors and warning radars) went to Tactical Air Command (TAC).

 **1946 - 1992**

 **1982 - present**

The ADC's communications and electronics assets went to the Air Force Communications Command (AFCC, now known as Air Force Communications Agency, AFCA). ADC's missile warning and space surveillance assets transferred to the Strategic Air Command (SAC) and then to the USAF Space Command in 1982.

1992 - present

 **1957 - present**

In 1992, the U.S. Air Force activated the Air Combat Command (ACC) and integrated the continental assets of SAC and TAC into this single operational command, while the Alaskan-based air defense resources fell under the Pacific Air Forces (PACAF).

1940 - present

1942- present

1975 - present

Today, the "alphabet soup" of the NORAD components includes US Air Combat Command forces (which operate under the First Air Force) and Pacific Air Forces (which operate under the Eleventh Air Force in Alaska), along with the 1 Canadian Air Division, which traces its lineage back to the establishment of Air Command Headquarters in Winnipeg in 1975.

THE NORAD BAND

Don Knotts, Lt. Col. Azzolina, Louis Nye and Col. Oldfield on the Steve Allen Show, 1960.

In today's world of iPods, MP3s, and downloading music, it is hard to remember how important bands—big bands with woodwinds, strings, brass, and percussion—were to music when NORAD took form. It is also hard to remember that NORAD not only played a defensive role, but also a musical one. On April 15, 1959, Colonel Barney Oldfield organized the NORAD Band: a 90-member unit drawn from US Army, US Air Force, US Navy, and Royal Canadian Air Force enlisted bandsmen. It was the only international, inter-service band ever in existence. The band premiered in Albuquerque, NM, and then set out on its first tour in the Pacific Northwest.

On the road, a NORAD Band Concert was the "Cavalcade of Music" with a focus on custom arrangements of show tunes and medleys. The band was in high demand and had appearances at the Canadian National Exhibition, the Michigan State Fair, and annual appearances at New York's Carnegie Hall. It also shot television spots on the *Bell Telephone Hour* and the *Dinah Shore Show*, culminating with an appearance on the *Steve Allen Show* in May 1960. In that year the American Federation of Musicians named the NORAD Band the "Honorary Best Band" at the annual Best Bands contest in Detroit.

In December 1964, Lieutenant Colonel Victor J. Molzer took over as director of the band, and in 1965, Captain Con Furey of the Canadian Armed Forces took up duties as assistant musical director. With a binational leadership, the NORAD Band continued a string of high-profile appearances for the command including Mexico City, the Hollywood Bowl, the New York's World Fair, Guatemala, EXPO 67 in Montreal, Iceland, the *Mike Douglas Show*, the *Today Show*, and the *Tonight Show*.

The Cavalcade also featured "The NORAD Commanders" jazz band. The Commanders' alumni list reads like a veritable "who's who" of successful musicians including Bobby Shew, Mike Whited, Bill Prince, Phil Wilson, Bobby Harriott, Warren Luening, Pete Rosa, Jerry Ash, Johnnie Zell, Richard Maloof, Kenny Kotwitz, Steve Bohannon, Jerry DeDad, Randy Aldcroft, Mike Brumbaugh, Clay Brandt, Jerry Liliedahl, Dave Wolpe, Larry Ford, Jim Straggari, Dave Edwards, Fred Hamilton, and Rick Drumm.

Off the road, the NORAD Band lived in a small barracks at Peterson Field, the airfield of Ent Air Force Base. The barracks were across from the rehearsal hall, which was conveniently located next to the NCO Club. One bandsman remembered that the club allowed the band to gather there "because they were such GREAT customers!!" NORAD band members were active on the local music scene with jam sessions at the "Cellar" in Manitou Springs and the "Emporium" in Colorado Springs. The band also recorded a number of albums including *Playback*, *About Faces*, *The NORAD Cavalcade of Music from Carnegie Hall*, *NORAD Night at Carnegie Hall*, *Exciting Sounds*, *Music from NORAD*, and *Ballads and Brass*.

The NORAD Band was retired in 1979 as each of the component bands went back to its respective service. The Air Force component was re-designated the 504th Air Force Band of the Golden Gate and moved to Travis Air Force Base, CA. It continues to perform as the United States Air Force Band of the Golden West. So the legacy of the NORAD Band, the "Cavalcade of Music," remains with us still.

Selected Readings for NORAD and Canadian-US Defense Relations

Bashow, David L. "The Changing Face of NORAD." *Proceedings* Nov. 95: 61-63.

Bouchard, Russel. "LE VILLAGE DE MONT-APICA: UNE BASE MILITAIRE DE LA NORAD, AU COEUR DE LA FORET BOREALE. (The village of Mont-Apica: a NORAD military base in the heart of the boreal forest.)" *Saguenayensia* 1999 41(2): 44-53.

Crosby, Ann Denholm. "A MIDDLE-POWER MILITARY IN ALLIANCE: CANADA AND NORAD." *Journal of Peace Research* 1997 34(1): 37-52.

—. *Dilemmas in defence decision-making:: constructing Canada's role in NORAD, 1958-96.* New York: St. Martin's, 1998.

Hebert, Adam J. "The Return of NORAD." *Air Force Magazine* Feb. 2002 (85.2): 50 (5 pp.).

Holman, D. Fraser. *NORAD in the new millennium.* Toronto, Canada: Irwin, 2000.

Jockel, Joseph T. "Canada in NORAD, 1957-2007: A History." *Queen's Policy Studies - School of Policy Studies, 28* Feb. 2008: n.p.

—. *No Boundaries Upstairs: Canada, the United States, and the Origins of North American Air Defence, 1945- 1958,* University of British Columbia Press, Vancouver, 1987.

Kilbourne, Lawrence J. and Thomas Fuller. "An Important Anniversary: Thirty Years of Successful U.S.-Canadian Partnership in NORAD." *Canadian Defence Quarterly* (Summer 1987): 36-40.

Lorden, Mike. "NORAD: Watchdog of the Skies." *World and I* Aug. 2002 (17.8): 46 (6 pp.).

New Mexico Engineering Research Institute. *NORAD's Cheyenne Mountain Combat Operations Center: The Cold War Years.* DOD Legacy Resource Management Program, August 1996.

"NORAD Leaders Through the Years." *Air Force Magazine* 2002 (85.5): 44.
"NORAD Leaders Through the Years." *Air Force Magazine* 2006 (89.5): 52.
"NORAD Leaders Through the Years." *Air Force Magazine* 2007 (90.5): 47.

Rossignol, Michael. *NORAD: Its History and its New Challenges [Background Paper BP-238E].* Ottawa: Library of Parliament, Research Branch, Sept. 1990.

Schaffel, Kenneth. *The Emerging Shield: The Air Force and the Evolution of Continental Air Defense, 1945-1960.* Washington, DC: Office of Air Force History, 1981.

Sokolsky, Joel J. *Defending Canada: U.S.-Canadian Defense Policies.* New York: Priority Press, 1989.

Sokolsky, Joel J. and Joseph T. Jockel. *Fifty Years of Canada- United States Defense Cooperation: The Road from Ogdensburg.* Lewiston, NY: Edwin Mellen Press, 1992.

Spencer, Lynn. *Touching history : the untold story of the drama that unfolded in the skies over America on 9/11.* New York: Free Press, 2008.

Talmadge, Marian T. and Iris Gilmore. *NORAD: The North American Air Defense Command.* New York: Dodd, Mead & Co., 1967.

50
NORAD

Guarding What You Value Most

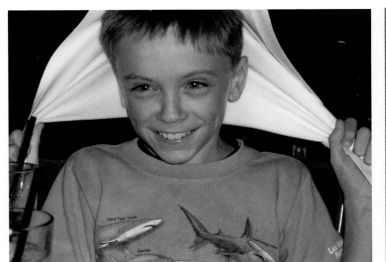

ABOUT THIS BOOK

Publisher
Michael B. Perini, ABC, Director
NORAD and USNORTHCOM Public Affairs

Senior Researcher
Dr. Thomas Fuller, Ph.D.
NORAD Historian

Editor
Major (USA) Thomas F. Veale, Ph.D.
Branch Chief, Cheyenne Mountain Mission Support/Public Affairs

Layout and Graphics
Staff Sergeant Christopher Sherrer, USAF
Cheyenne Mountain Mission Support/Graphics

All photographs in this book that are not property the United States or Canada are either used by permission or fall under no copyright protection. Special thanks to the combat camera crews, military photographers, and graphics shops of both nations and all commands.

Students of the University of Nebraska's College of Journalism and Mass Communication program brainstormed what NORAD means to Canadians and Americans and proposed the slogan we are using throughout our celebration: Guarding What You Value Most. Staff Sergeant Michael Schwartz created the 50th Anniversary logo.

This book was published through the Defense Logistics Agency's Document Automation & Production Service (DAPS) and the US Government Printing Office (GPO). We would like to thank Jim Westover at the US Air Force Academy DAPS Office and David Goldberg at the Seattle GPO Office for their time, effort, and expertise.

 Additional copies may be available for purchase directly from the GPO or through the NORAD Kit Shop at Peterson AFB, CO.

There are several options for ordering through the GPO:
To order in person: visit the GPO Bookstore at 710 North Capitol Street N.W. / Washington, DC between 8:00 a.m. and 4:30 p.m. EST.
To order online: visit the U.S. Government Online Bookstore at http://bookstore.gpo.gov
To order by phone: call toll-free 866.512.1800 or, in the Washington, D.C. metro area, call 202.512.1800 from 7:00 a.m.- 9:00 p.m. EST.
To order by fax: dial 202.512.2104.
To order by e-mail: send order inquiries to contactcenter@gpo.gov
All orders require prepayment by VISA, MasterCard, American Express, or Discover/NOVUS credit cards, check, or SOD deposit account.

Contact the GPO's Superintendent of Documents at P.O. Box 37954 / Pittsburgh, PA 15250-7954

To order through the NORAD Kit Shop, please send e-mail to NORAD50@NORAD.MIL or visit http://www.cmfrc-colorado.com/50th/KitShop.html

NORAD 50th ANNIVERSARY COMMITTEE

Colonel Richard Dunstan (NORAD HQ/J5): Co-chair
William Gessner (NORAD HQ Chief of Staff's Office): Co-chair
Michael Perini (NORAD HQ Public Affairs): Co-Chair

Major Jessica "Meg" Baker (NORAD HQ/J35): NORAD Kit Shop and NORAD Commemorative Time Capsule
Joyce Frankovis (NORAD HQ Public Affairs): Committee Administrative Assistant
Dr. Thomas Fuller (NORAD HQ/HO): NORAD Historian
Patricia Goude (NORAD HQ/HO): NORAD Historian's Office Representative
Lieutenant Colonel John Grady (NORAD HQ/J33): Stakeholder Involvement (fundraising and volunteers)
Master Sergeant Anthony Hill (NORAD HQ Public Affairs): Media Engagement Coordinator
Lieutenant (Navy) Wilfred Hutchings (NORAD HQ/J6): NORAD 50th Anniversary Webmaster
Doug Johnson (US Political Advisor's Office): Airport Advertisements Coordinator
Major James Kennedy (NORAD HQ/JA): Legal Advisor
Nathalie Lachance (NORAD HQ Public Affairs): NORAD Commemorative Time Capsule
Lieutenant (Junior Grade) Ryan Lally (Cheyenne Mountain/PA): NORAD Commemorative Time Capsule
Staff Sergeant Bonnie Lame Bull (NORAD HQ/J33): NORAD Kit Shop

Captain Laurie Lanpher (NORAD HQ/J8): Budget Manager
Brian Lihani: Colorado NORAD License Plate and Pro-Stock Car
Captain Craig Marsh (NORAD HQ/CP): Command Protocol
Lieutenant Colonel Michael Price (NORAD HQ/J4): NORAD Ball Coordinator and US Army Engineer Liaison
Major Jason Proulx (NORAD HQ Public Affairs): Anniversary Project Manager
Major Kenn Rodzinyak (NORAD HQ/CX): Federal Engagement (US and Canada)
Captain Mike Rogers (NORAD HQ/J3): NORAD Time Capsule
Major Derek Salley (NORAD HQ/J5): HQ NORAD Picnic
Major Casey Saunders (NORAD HQ/J5): HQ NORAD Picnic
Chief Master Sergeant Barbara Savage (NORAD HQ/NG): National Guard Office Liaison
Staff Sergeant Michael Schwartz (NORAD HQ/Command Graphics): Graphic Designs
Lieutenant Colonel Kristine Shelstad (NORAD HQ/IA): Letters to State Governors
Staff Sergeant Christopher Sherrer (Cheyenne Mountain/Graphics): NORAD Book Layout and Design
Wynn Anne Sibbald (NORAD HQ Public Affairs): Marketing, Displays, Translations and Liaison
Major Thomas Veale (Cheyenne Mountain/PA): NORAD Book Editor
Laurie White (NORAD HQ/CP): Command Protocol
Shelley Whiting (Canadian Political Advisor's Office): Canadian Federal/Provincial Engagement

Others who contributed to the NORAD 50th Anniversary

Lieutenant Colonel Don Arias: Continental US NORAD Region Public Affairs
Lieutenant Colonel Almarah Belk (Pentagon/PA): NORAD Liaison
Karen Christiuk: Canadian NORAD Region Public Affairs
Major Allen Herritage: Alaska NORAD Region Public Affairs
John Knoll (NDHQ ADM/PA): NORAD 50th Anniversary Coordinator
Master Sergeant Karin Krause: Alaska NORAD Region Public Affairs
Ms. Anne Marshall (President, Isis Company): Producer of the NORAD Jubilee Ball

Captain Steve Neta: Canadian NORAD Region Public Affairs
Lieutenant Colonel Nancy Ouellet (Canadian Forces Support Unit): Event Advisor
Lieutenant Colonel Erik Stor (US Army 4th ENG Bn, Fort Carson): NORAD Time Capsule
Alvin Strait (21st Space Wing, PAFB): 21st SW Liaison to the NORAD 50th Anniversary Committee
Maureen Villeneuve (NDHQ ADM/PA): NORAD 50th Anniversary Coordinator
Joe Wiggins: Continental US NORAD Region Public Affairs

WWW.NORAD.MIL
North American Aerospace Defense Command
Deter. Detect. Defend.

Guarding What You Value Most

Gardien de ce qui vous tient à coeur

50 NORAD